ALL THE
LITTLE THINGS,
as observed by

_____

_____

EXTRAORDINARY OBJECTS

········ ## OBJECTS ········

OBSERVER'S JOURNAL

See the Small and Appreciate It All

· · · · · · · · · · · · · · · · · · · ·

Illustrated by Jenny Bowers

CHRONICLE BOOKS

SAN FRANCISCO

JENNY BOWERS is an illustrator based in London who creates vibrant artwork using paper, paint, and pencils. A member of the UK–based illustration collective Peepshow, she works collaboratively and independently on products ranging from stationery to textiles for clients around the world.
www.peepshow.org.uk

• •

ISBN: 978-1-4521-3728-5

Manufactured in China

Text by Jay Sacher
Design by Kristen Hewitt
Typeset in Escrow Condensed and Ultra Regular

10 9 8 7 6 5 4 3 2 1

Chronicle Books LLC
680 Second Street
San Francisco, CA 94107
www.chroniclebooks.com

HOW EXTRAORDINARY, THE ORDINARY

William Carlos Williams, the great poet—and master of understanding the power of little, everyday things—wrote in his 1923 poem, "XXII," "so much depends / upon / a red wheel / barrow / glazed with rain / water / beside the white / chickens."

It's a powerful idea, the notion of being delighted just by the details.

The prompts in this journal are designed to help you notice and celebrate the little things in life that make up the backbeat to our days. It could be as simple as thinking about a cherished piece of clothing in a new light, or focusing on the power of color, or listening to the hum of conversation in the room around you. The prompts may inspire you to sketch or to write or to make lists. When we take the time to examine the objects and compositions around us as if each were a work of art—if we hold them up to the light, contemplate and cherish them—we start to see how much truly does depend on them. After all, they make up our lives. They add color and music and joy. Spend some time with the world around you.

Start small. And have fun.

LET'S OBSERVE.

WHAT ARE YOU WRITING THIS WITH?
Tell the story of your writing tool.

FOCUS ON A SINGLE COLOR IN THE SPACE AROUND YOU.

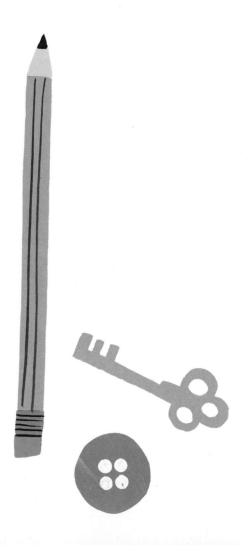

*Catalog it here in all its visible iterations,
from the big dominant hues to the tiniest accents.*

WHAT OBJECT IN YOUR HOME REMINDS YOU MOST OF FAMILY?

CATALOG, *in words or pictures,*
THE CONTENTS OF YOUR POCKETS,
HANDBAG, *or* KNAPSACK.

JOT DOWN RANDOM WORDS YOU SEE FROM
WHERE YOU'RE SITTING.

Do they combine to make new meaning, a poem, or a message?

FIND SOMETHING THAT HAS BEEN
OVERLOOKED, DISCARDED, *or* ABANDONED.

Catalog it here.

IS THAT STAPLER STARING AT YOU?
IS THAT PENDANT SMILING?

What inanimate faces can you find?

POLKA DOTS *or* STRIPES?

OBJECTS CAN BE UNINTENTIONALLY
ARRANGED WITH SUCH ELEGANCE AND
APLOMB—a pile of change on a countertop,

a collection of spoons
in a kitchen jar.

What accidental arrangements strike you as lovely?

FIND SOMETHING THAT'S
BEAUTIFUL TO YOU.

Catalog it here.

SEEK OUT TRIPTYCHS IN YOUR
SURROUNDINGS.

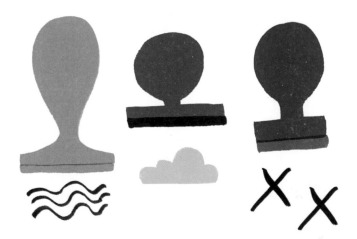

*What objects, ideas, people,
or other items seem to travel in threes?*

SEARCH FOR THE ALPHABET OUTSIDE OF THE WRITTEN WORD.

Do you see an Λ in the crossed branches of a tree? An M in the handles of a shopping bag? List any accidental alphabets you come across.

SEARCH OUT "LINKS"—THICK LIKE
A BICYCLE LOCK, DELICATE LIKE A
NECKLACE.

Where is one thing linked to another?

FOCUS ON A SINGLE COLOR IN
THE SPACE AROUND YOU.

Catalog it here in all its visible iterations,
from the big dominant hues to the tiniest accents.

WHAT SONG PERFECTLY CAPTURES THIS MOMENT?

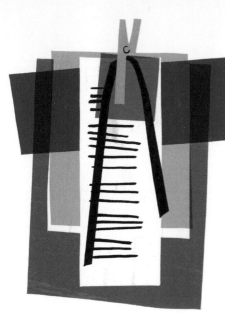

PAPERCLIPS,
CLOTHESPINS,
STAPLES,
TAPE:

Write about a particularly captivating example of how these everyday items marry one object to another.

CHOOSE AN ITEM IN YOUR HOME THAT EMBODIES HAPPINESS.
What does it look like?

FIND SOMETHING THAT HAS BEEN
OVERLOOKED, DISCARDED, *or* ABANDONED.

Catalog it here.

YESTERDAY *or* TOMORROW?

WHICH BOOKS DO YOU CHERISH?
Describe their qualities, inside and out.

CHOOSE AN ITEM IN YOUR HOME THAT EMBODIES COMFORT. *What does it look like?*

FIND SOMETHING THAT'S
BEAUTIFUL TO YOU.

Catalog it here.

WHAT IS YOUR TOTEM—ONE POSSESSION
THAT SAYS SOMETHING ABOUT YOUR SPIRIT
AND CHARACTER? *Describe it here.*

DRAW A FEW RANDOM LINES ON THIS PAGE.

Now look around the space you're in.

IF YOU HAD TO PAIR YOUR
MARKS WITH SOMETHING
IN THE ROOM, *what would it
be and why?*

OBSERVE YOUR SURROUNDINGS AS IF YOU WERE A FILM DIRECTOR. *What kind of movie would suit the tableau?*

Describe it here: its sights, sounds, genre, colors, and mood.

FOCUS ON A SINGLE COLOR IN THE SPACE
AROUND YOU.

Catalog it here in all its visible iterations,
from the big dominant hues to the tiniest accents.

PICK A BELOVED OBJECT FROM YOUR HOME
and write a custom description for it as if it were to be sold at auction.

LOOK AT AN OLD PHOTOGRAPH OF
YOURSELF FROM CHILDHOOD. *What
memories does that image conjure?*

IS YOUR PHONE NEW AND SHINING *or* OLD AND CRACKED?

Does it have battered charm or a covetable case?

FIND SOMETHING THAT HAS BEEN
OVERLOOKED, DISCARDED, *or* ABANDONED.

Catalog it here.

SUNRISE *or* SUNSET?

OPEN TO A RANDOM PAGE OF A DICTIONARY
AND STOP ON THE FIRST ADJECTIVE YOU SEE.

(adjective)

Find an item within view that fits that adjective and describe why this is so.

LIST YOUR TEN MOST PRIZED POSSESSIONS.

1.

2.

3.

4.

5.

6.

7.

8.

9.

10.

IF YOU HAD TO GIVE AWAY ALL BUT ONE,
WHICH WOULD YOU KEEP *and why?*

FIND SOMETHING THAT'S
BEAUTIFUL TO YOU.

Catalog it here.

WHAT ARE THE MOST BEAUTIFUL
IMPERFECTIONS—SCRATCHES, DENTS,
PATINA, DECAY—IN THE OBJECTS
AROUND YOU?

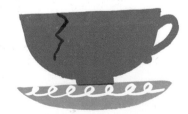

SEARCH FOR RECTANGLES—IN THE PLAID OF
A FABRIC, IN BRICKWORK, ON THE PAGES OF A
MAGAZINE. *How do they visually interact with one
another?*

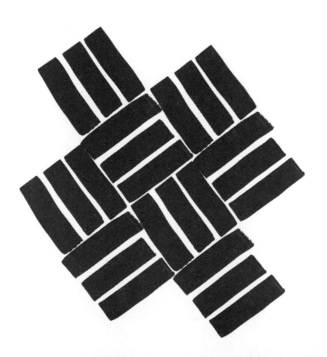

THINK ABOUT THE ART ON THE WALL.

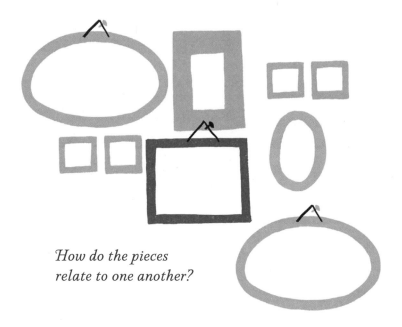

*How do the pieces
relate to one another?*

FOCUS ON A SINGLE COLOR IN THE SPACE
AROUND YOU.

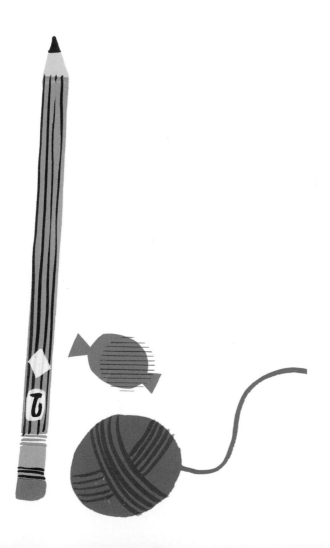

Catalog it here in all its visible iterations,
from the big dominant hues to the tiniest accents.

PATTERNS ARE EVERYWHERE—IN NATURE,
IN FASHION, IN ART. CONSIDER A PATTERN
WITHIN VIEW OF WHERE YOU'RE SITTING.
Can you re-create it here, either literally or
figuratively?

EXPLORE THE BEAUTY OF INDUSTRIAL
OBJECTS: AN AUTOMOBILE, A TELEPHONE,
AN ESPRESSO MACHINE.

Write about the quality of these objects.

SUNLIGHT *or* MOONLIGHT?

FIND SOMETHING THAT HAS BEEN
OVERLOOKED, DISCARDED, *or* ABANDONED.

Catalog it here.

WHAT ARE YOU NOT?
FIND THE OBJECT IN YOUR SURROUNDINGS
THAT IS THE EXACT OPPOSITE OF WHAT
EMBODIES YOUR CHARACTER.

Explore why this is so.

WHAT TIME OF DAY IS IT?

Catalog all the ways in which the time affects your surroundings, from sights and sounds to aromas and your own mood.

THINK ABOUT NEGATIVE SPACE.
What are the shapes that exist between the objects around you?

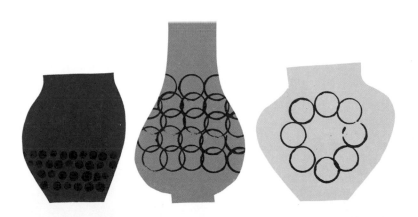

FIND SOMETHING THAT'S
BEAUTIFUL TO YOU.

Catalog it here.

IS THERE
BEAUTY
IN THE
PATTERNS
BENEATH
OUR FEET?

THE TILE WORK, THE WOOD, OR THE GRAIN OF THE CEMENT—*imagine how it would appear if it were a textile.*

WHAT IS THE OLDEST THING IN THE SPACE AROUND YOU?

Catalog it here.

WHAT IS THE NEWEST ITEM IN THE SPACE AROUND YOU? *Catalog it here.*

FOCUS ON A SINGLE COLOR IN THE SPACE
AROUND YOU.

Catalog it here in all its visible iterations,
from the big dominant hues to the tiniest accents.

SEARCH FOR YOUR FAVORITE HANDMADE OBJECT IN YOUR IMMEDIATE VICINITY.

What makes it unique?

WHAT IS THE SMALLEST OBJECT YOU CAN
FIND IN THE SPACE AROUND YOU?

Where is it? Why is it there?

_____

_____

_____

_____

_____

_____

What is it made of?

_____

_____

_____

_____

_____

_____

_____

_____

FIND SOMETHING THAT HAS BEEN
OVERLOOKED, DISCARDED, *or* ABANDONED.

Catalog it here.

ORDER *or* DISARRAY?

JOT DOWN THE FIRST FIVE WORDS THAT
COME TO MIND WHEN YOU OBSERVE THE
SPACE AROUND YOU.

1.

2.

3.

4.

5.

Take the word from that list that interests you the most and delve deeper into how it connects to your surroundings.

SEARCH YOUR SURROUNDINGS FOR
KNOTTED OBJECTS: TWINE, TASSELS,
LACES, ROPE. *Describe them, from their colors
to their shapes to their strength and uses.*

HOW MANY MILES HAVE YOU WALKED IN THE SHOES ON YOUR FEET? *Where have they been? Where do you want them to go?*

_____

_____

_____

_____

_____

_____

_____

_____

_____

_____

_____

_____

_____

_____

_____

_____

_____

_____

_____

_____

_____

_____

FIND SOMETHING THAT'S
BEAUTIFUL TO YOU.

Catalog it here.

WHERE DO YOU STASH YOUR CASH?

Tell the story of this everyday item: its age, its color, its importance to you.

FIND THE MOST ORDINARY ITEM YOU CAN IN THE SPACE AROUND YOU.

_____

(item)

TRY TO MAP OUT ALL THE THOUGHT THAT
WENT INTO CREATING THIS OBJECT, FROM
ITS DESIGN TO ITS PRODUCTION.

List as many details as you can think of.

GIVE YOURSELF SYNESTHESIA.

Try to describe what the sounds you hear around you might look like: their colors, their shapes, their characters.

FOCUS ON A SINGLE COLOR IN THE SPACE
AROUND YOU.

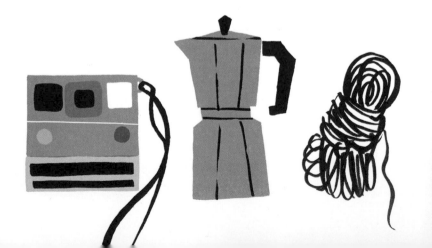

Catalog it here in all its visible iterations,
from the big dominant hues to the tiniest accents.

WHICH COMPLEMENTARY COLORS
—RED-GREEN, YELLOW-VIOLET,
BLUE-ORANGE—SURROUND YOU IN
OUTFITS, PATTERNS, *and* OBJECTS?

WHAT'S THE MOST RECENT GIFT YOU'VE RECEIVED?

Does it have any special significance for you?

WE ARE SURROUNDED BY LOGOS—IN
ADVERTISING AND ON PRODUCTS.

Which ones do you see?

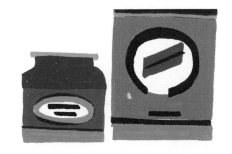

FIND SOMETHING THAT HAS BEEN
OVERLOOKED, DISCARDED, *or* ABANDONED.

Catalog it here.

FROM FIGURINES TO ILLUSTRATIONS
TO JEWELRY *or* STATUES, SEARCH OUT
REPRESENTATIONS OF ANIMAL LIFE
IN THE SPACE AROUND YOU.

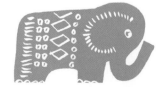

Which ones work?
Which ones fall flat?

PATTERNS *or* SOLIDS?

FIND PAIRINGS IN YOUR HOME
OR SURROUNDINGS.

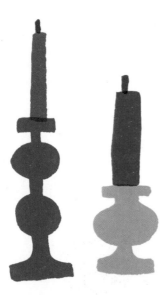

What duos of objects, people, or sights work in tandem, either by contrasting with or complementing one another?

FIND SOMETHING THAT'S
BEAUTIFUL TO YOU.

Catalog it here.

CONSIDER YOUR IDEAL DESKTOP.
IT CAN BE AT WORK OR HOME OR
ELSEWHERE. *What's on it?*

CATALOG THE TOOLS IN YOUR HOME.

Where did they come from? When did you last use them?

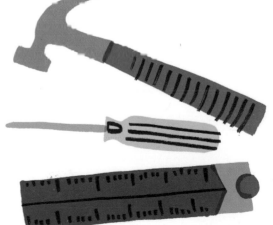

WHAT SEASON IS IT RIGHT NOW?

How is the space around you affected by the season?

List all the ways you can find, from sounds to sights to aromas.

FOCUS ON A SINGLE COLOR IN
THE SPACE AROUND YOU.

Catalog it here in all its visible iterations,
from the big dominant hues to the tiniest accents.

SEARCH FOR ASYMMETRY IN THE OBJECTS AND SIGHTS AROUND YOU.

What's askew or off-kilter?

WHAT WAS YOUR FAVORITE TOY AS A CHILD? *Describe it here.*

FIND SOMETHING THAT HAS BEEN OVERLOOKED, DISCARDED, *or* ABANDONED.

Catalog it here.

SEARCH FOR AN OBJECT THAT WOULD MAKE
A GORGEOUS PATTERN. IT CAN
BE ANYTHING—A FORK, A RING, A
PINECONE. *Describe or draw it here.*

NOW THE REVERSE: FIND A COVETABLE
PATTERN AND APPLY IT TO AN OBJECT.
Describe it. Why does it captivate you?

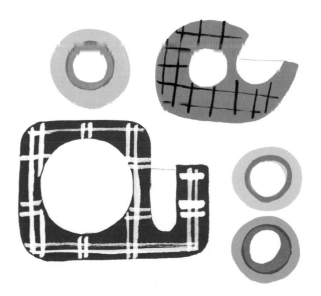

WHAT IS THE MOST VERSATILE OBJECT YOU OWN?

How many different ways do you use it?

Is it beautiful or functional, or both?

IF THE SPACE YOU ARE IN RIGHT
NOW WERE A MUSEUM, WHAT TYPE
OF MUSEUM WOULD IT BE?

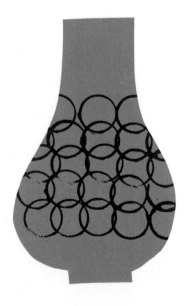

What object around you would become an artifact in the distant future, prized by generations to come?

FIND SOMETHING THAT'S
BEAUTIFUL TO YOU.

Catalog it here.

The End.